DYING TO KNOW...

About Death, Funeral Customs, and Final Resting Places

Dying to Know...

About Death, Funeral Customs, and Final Resting Places

LILA PERL

TWENTY-FIRST CENTURY BOOKS   BROOKFIELD, CONNECTICUT

Photographs courtesy of Stock Montage, Inc.: pp. 10 (© Charles Walker Collection), 11, 23, 48, 65; AP/Wide World Photos: p. 12; © Corbis/Bettmann: pp. 13, 25, 27, 40; Library of Congress: pp. 15, 73, 75 (top), 81; Culver Pictures, Inc.: pp. 16, 22; The Granger Collection, New York: pp. 17, 35, 38 (top); North Wind Picture Archives: pp. 20, 60; Woodfin Camp & Associates: pp. 21 (© Jehangir Gazdar), 37 (© *The Washington Post* 1978/Frank Johnston), 80; NGS Image Collection: pp. 26 (© Stephen Alvarez), 28 (© O. Louis Mazzatenta), 41 (© Nathan Benn); Photo Edit: pp. 31 (© Bill Aron), 33 (© Tom McCarthy), 34 (© Michael Newman); Corbis: p. 66 (© Kevin Fleming); Philadelphia Museum of Art: Gift of the Barra Foundation, Inc.: p. 44; Liaison Agency/Hulton Getty: pp. 46, 47 (bottom), 62; National Museum of Funeral History/Gary L. Sanders: p. 47 (top); Liaison Agency: pp. 55 (© Shahn Kermani), 57 (© Shahn Kermani), 82 (© Seymour Linden/FDB); The National Archives: p. 53; Lucinda Dowell: p. 54; Edward Owen/Art Resource, NY: p. 63; Phototheque Músees de la Ville de Paris/Carnavalet : p. 64; Museum of City of NY: p. 68; E. Parker Hayden, Jr. and Nancy Ellis: p. 70; Special Collections Room, Glendale Public Library, California: p. 71; Photo Collection/Los Angeles Public Library: p. 75 (bottom); American Antiquarian Society: p. 78; © Association for Gravestone Studies: p. 79.

Library of Congress Cataloging-in-Publication Data
Perl, Lila.
Dying to know—about death, funeral customs, and final resting places /
by Lila Perl.
p. cm.
Includes bibliographical references and index.
ISBN 0-7613-1564-0 (lib. bdg.)
1. Funeral rites and ceremonies—Juvenile literature. 2. Death—Cross-cultural studies—Juvenile literature. 3. Cemeteries—Cross-cultural studies—Juvenile
literature. [1. Funeral rites and ceremonies. 2. Cemeteries.]
GT3150 .P45 2001   393—dc21   2001016166

Published by Twenty-First Century Books
A Division of The Millbrook Press, Inc.
2 Old New Milford Road
Brookfield, Connecticut 06804
www.millbrookpress.com

To all who've survived death...
through loving memory

Contents

1

The Mystery at the End of Life

ALL YOU WHO PASSETH BY,
AS YOU ARE NOW, SO WAS I.
AS I AM NOW, SO YOU WILL BE,
PREPARE FOR DEATH AND FOLLOW ME.

This verse from a 1775 New England tombstone, grim though it is, is a reminder of a universal truth: All who live must die. Life and death are eternally entwined. One cannot exist without the other, and it is perhaps the inevitability of death that gives the gift of life its richness, its zest, and its quest for fulfillment.

Yet there are many ways of looking at death. Although it is an everyday occurrence everywhere, most people in Western society today do not like to think about it. Death may, in fact, be the last taboo, the specter that we'd rather not encounter face-to-face.

On the other hand, there have been and still are groups in society who embrace death, who see it as a continuation of life not only in a spiritual sense but also as a somewhat mysterious physical manifestation.

9

The ancient Egyptians went to great lengths to preserve their dead in a mummified state, believing that the existence of the body guaranteed an eternal life of the soul, a soul that might want to eat and drink, and enjoy games and sport, in the afterlife. So they provided their dead with tomb goods of many kinds and even with servants in the form of wood or pottery figurines known as *shabtis*, or "answerers."

An outstanding example of loving intimacy with the departed that is still practiced today is the Mexican Day of the Dead, which is observed on November 1 and 2, All Saints' Day and All Souls' Day on the Christian calendar.

While young people in the United States and Canada are ringing doorbells on Halloween, October 31, dressed as ghosts, witches, skeletons, and other bizarre and eerie characters, Mexicans are visiting their families' graves bringing the favorite foods and drink of the deceased, candles and incense, and bouquets of marigolds, the "flowers of the dead." The graveside picnics are "shared" by the dead and the living, and are often extended into overnight vigils.

Instead of going trick-or-treating, Mexican children exchange special holiday confections—cakes and candies decorated with skulls and skeletons fashioned out of sugar frosting. Although the death's heads may be grinning, they are also playful. They don't convey the idea that the spirits of the dead are evil and threatening, as in the typical trappings of Halloween. Day of the Dead ceremonies are also observed in parts of Central and South America.

While death is the mystery at the end of life, it does not necessarily arrive in old age. Although life spans are increasing in the more socially and industrially advanced parts of the world, new scourges seem to come along all the time. People

The Mexican Day of the Dead, sometimes known as La Fiesta de los Muertos, calls for the preparation of crude but fanciful images of death in the form of skeletons.

Wanting to remain close to the departed seems to span time and place. This group is having tea, assumedly among deceased relatives, at Smolensky Cemetery in St. Petersburg, Russia in 1881.

in poorer and less developed regions have always had shorter life expectancies, mainly due to infectious and parasitic diseases. And they can be annihilated in the millions by epidemics such as AIDS (a disease of the immune system), which kill off adults in their prime, leaving behind children who may well not reach their own maturity unless massive efforts are made to halt the disease.

Accidents, too, play a major role in cutting off life before it has run its course. In the United States, traffic accidents are the leading cause of such deaths, mounting to more than 42,000 per year, while worldwide at least 175,000 individuals die every year as a result of motor vehicle crashes.

When death does come with advanced age, it usually tells us that the individual has benefited from a supportive environment, a healthful lifestyle, good genes, and very often just plain luck.

Although scientific studies report that theoretically we should be able to live to the age of 115 to 120, few of us do. Disregarding claims for longevity that cannot be proven, records show that the oldest known person to have lived was a Frenchwoman named Jeanne Calment, who reached the age of 122. Mme. Calment, who was born in Arles, France, on February 21, 1875, even acted in a movie when she was 114. The film, made in Canada and released in 1990, was about the painter Vincent van Gogh, and was titled *Vincent and Me*. Jeanne Calment died in August 1997.

A runner-up, following the death of Mme. Calment, was a Pennsylvania woman named Sarah Knauss, who died on December 30, 1999, having reached the age of 119. Ms. Knauss was born on September 24, 1880, and had she survived two days more she would have attained the distinction of having lived in three centuries.

Jeanne Calment is pictured in The Guinness Book of World Records at the age of 120, two years before her death.

Whether we die young or old, in health or sickness, death itself remains a mystery. How, in fact, can we even be sure that the newly dead are truly incapable of being revived?

In an earlier day, fears of live burial were widespread, and all sorts of precautions were taken to avoid such a catastrophe. Since the late 1960s, however, medical science has taken steps to measure brain function rather than pulse or breathing stoppage as the determining factor in declaring a patient dead. Thus a complete set of brain activity criteria is employed by

An undated painting depicts the horror of awakening in a casket after having been assumed to be dead. The victim, though, has the advantage of being in an underground vault rather than buried beneath the earth.

physicians and hospital personnel. Such a verification of death is especially important today when technology has made it possible for machines to keep a patient's heart pumping blood and the lungs breathing air.

Among the hideous tales of live burial are those that describe the discovery of corpses in tortured positions, with arms and legs flung about as a result of trying to pry open the lid of the coffin. And there have even been reports of grave robbers being welcomed with relief by the recently "deceased."

During the 1800s, one inventor went so far as to come up with a trumpetlike speaking tube connecting the interior of the coffin with the cemetery grounds, so that calls of distress from below might easily be heard. There was even a device invented that would activate a system of jangling bells and waving flags to call attention to the plight of a "living" corpse.

The first president of the United States shared the widespread fear of a live burial. Just before George Washington died at his home, Mount Vernon, on December 14, 1799, he said: "I am just going." Then he added his last request: "Have me decently buried, and do not let my body be put in the vault in less than two days after I am dead. Do you understand me?"

Washington's message was clearly understood. Nor was it unusual for the dying to ask for much more extreme precautions against live burial, such as having the soles of one's feet scratched with a razor, one's heart pierced with a needle, or even having one's head cut off.

In the second half of the 1800s, during the American Civil War, the fear of premature burial was erased through the introduction of a modern form of embalming. In this process, the blood and other body fluids were drained and a preservative was injected into the arteries. As a result, bodies did not decay as rapidly, making it possible for the war dead to be shipped home from the battlefields. Embalming also permitted the deceased to remain on view for a longer period of time, and, of course, it ensured the finality of death.

But not all religions or individuals were to accept this practice. When Eleanor Roosevelt, the wife of President Franklin Roosevelt, died in 1962, she left strict instructions for the disposal of her body. She was to be buried in a plain wooden coffin covered with pine boughs and, as she did not wish to be embalmed, she left orders that her veins were to be cut.

 A mystery about death that persists—even in the age of modern science—is the question of what happens to us after

A rare Civil War photograph shows a surgeon pumping embalming fluid into a soldier's body.

the last breath leaves the body, after the final vestige of brain activity has ceased. We know that the physical body begins to decompose. But where is the personhood, where are the thoughts and feelings, the experiences and awarenesses that make each of us a unique being? A variety of religious and spiritual beliefs try to respond to this question. But the answer remains elusive for many of us.

Because death is such a mystery, attempts have long been made to visualize it, often in human or animal form. It has been spoken of as "the grim reaper," a figure in a black hood and cloak carrying a scythe. Sometimes, as described in the New Testament, death appears in a ghostly light: "And I looked, and behold a pale horse: and his name that sat on him was Death."

An etching depicting the
mythological ferryman
Charon transporting
souls over the River Styx
to Hades

This manuscript drawing of Cerberus dates
from the 1500s. Only the Greek hero
Hercules was able to overcome the beast.
With his great strength, he brought
Cerberus to the King of Argos, and then
returned him to the underworld.

In ancient Greek lore, death was a "boatman," a gruff
old man named Charon, who ferried the dead across the
River Styx to a place called Hades. The Greeks placed a
bronze coin beneath the corpse's tongue as payment of the
fare that Charon demanded. And often they included a
honey cake for Cerberus, the three-headed dog that
guarded the gates of Hades.

But no matter how death has been visualized over the
ages, its true nature has always challenged the living.
Horace, the ancient Greek poet, assured us that none come

back "from Hades' shore." But it was Shakespeare who put it best when he wrote that death is:

> THE UNDISCOVER'D COUNTRY
> FROM WHOSE BOURN
> NO TRAVELER RETURNS . . .

Whether we avoid thoughts of death or face up to it realistically through religious faith or other means, its inevitability is still hard to accept. So it's not surprising to learn that some early peoples believed that there was a time when death did not exist, and they wove legends to explain how death came to be.

An old African tale tells us about the time before there was death. God gave Toad a clay jar, warning him that he must be very careful not to break it. Toad wondered why, and God explained that the jar contained Death.

Toad went on his way, very carefully protecting the fragile jar. But soon he met Frog. Frog begged Toad to let him carry the jar for a while, so Toad gave it to him with God's warning. But Frog was careless. He began to skip and hop about so wildly that the jar fell and broke. Out flew Death, and ever since we have all had to deal with this fact of life.

2

Funeral Customs:
Among Prehistoric
and Ancient Peoples

Prehistoric peoples lived intimately with death. Its ravages were everywhere and life was truly short and violent. The causes of death were usually obvious—cold, hunger, a fall while out hunting, an attack by a wild beast. But why did some people die from exposure and injury and others not? What if death were a disease? What if it were catching?

So, often, the first instinct was to distance oneself from death. For the hunting peoples of prehistory, a funeral might consist of placing the bodies of the deceased in a cave or other natural shelter before the group, of necessity, moved on to other hunting grounds. Sometimes a little food and a few tools were left in the cave. The living felt that these would provide the deceased with everyday comforts to which they'd become accustomed.

In this woodcut, a group of Sioux Indians offers gifts to a dead comrade.

For other groups, the disposal of the dead took a different form. Instead of cave burials, they chose exposure to animals, birds, or the elements. They did this by placing the bodies in the tops of trees or on specially built log platforms. Soon nature would take its course, and the corpses would be reduced to a heap of bones. This type of exposure was practiced by the Aborigines of Australia and by some Native American peoples. In polar climates, the dead could simply be put out on the ice to become food for wolves, and some cultures even accepted the practice of abandoning living but old and useless members of society to the elements to freeze to death.

The Parsis, followers of an ancient Persian prophet named Zoroaster, adopted exposure of the dead as a tenet of their religion. They believed that a corpse would defile the sacred elements of earth, fire, and water if it were buried, burned, or drowned. So they built Towers of Silence, round stone towers, about 30 feet (9 meters) high, atop hills far away from the city.

The bodies of the dead were carried up into these towers and placed on stone slabs or iron gratings. Often it took less than an hour for a body to be picked clean by vultures or other birds of prey. The bones would then dry and drop through to the bottom of the tower where a pit had been dug to receive them.

The outlines of the Parsis' Towers of Silence can be seen today in India. Urban sprawl has surrounded the once-isolated sites, now visited more by tourists than by mourners.

After Persia was conquered by the Muslims in the seventh century A.D., many Parsis moved to India so that they could continue to practice their religion. Parsis still live there today, especially in and around the city of Bombay.

Among the ancient Romans, there was a deep-seated fear of the dead returning to life. So as soon as death occurred, they called out the name of the deceased loudly three times. Then they waited as long as eight or nine days before disposing of the body. Wealthy Romans, who could afford the scarce and costly wood for a funeral pyre, followed the Greek custom of cremation. Roman citizens of lesser means were buried directly in the ground.

When a cremation took place, the Romans were careful to seal the door of the house through which the body had been removed and to devise a round-about route to the outdoor crematory ground. They even scattered thorns on the return path to make sure that the ghost of the dead could not return. The ashes of prosperous and powerful Romans were kept in elaborate urns and placed in niches in homes and temples.

As the supply of wood grew ever scarcer, underground galleries known as catacombs were dug outside the city walls. Many of the early Christians were buried in the catacombs, where their bodies gradually became skeletal remains. The catacombs of ancient Rome, along the road known as the Appian Way, can still be visited today.

While so many early peoples feared death and wanted to put it far away from them, there were also those who cherished the dead. Once prehistoric societies began to practice agriculture, it became customary to bury the dead in the earth. Aside from wanting to keep the dead nearby, some groups even practiced cannibalism, consuming parts of the body as a way of taking on the strength and virtues of the departed. In fact, crushed skulls have even been found among the remains of Peking man, who lived in China during the Old Stone Age. It is believed that the skulls were shattered so that the living could partake of the brains of the dead.

Of all ancient peoples, none took more care with the bodies of the nonliving than the Egyptians. Unlike their neighbors in southwest Asia—the Assyrians and the Babylonians, who did not preserve their dead or believe in an afterlife—the ancient Egyptians went to great lengths to make mummies.

It was almost by accident that the earliest dwellers along the Nile discovered mummification. They found that when they buried their dead in the desert sands that lay beyond the

The ancient Egyptian process of embalming was an elaborate one. As the layers of bandages were applied, warm melted resin was poured over them to harden into a coating that would prevent moisture from entering the body.

23

riverbank, the bodies would dry out so rapidly that they would not decay. In fact, a body dug up from its dry-sand grave, after a long time had passed, might be darkened and leathery, but it would still be recognizable as the person it had once been.

To preserve their dead, and especially their great rulers, for eternity, the Egyptians found a way to make mummies without depending on nature. They did this by removing the organs that decayed easily, such as the lungs, liver, stomach, and intestines. In later times, they also removed the brain and sometimes the heart.

The most important step in this form of ancient embalming was the drying out of the body by coating it inside and out with a powdery white salt called natron. This salt was plentiful in the Egyptian desert.

After thirty-five to forty days, the salt drew the moisture out of the body. The dried-out body was then perfumed with spices, wrapped in linen, and ornamented according to its former station in life. It took as long as seventy days to prepare a royal Egyptian mummy for burial in a great pyramid or rock-cut tomb.

Ordinary Egyptians were also mummified. But their bodies were generally buried in mass graves rather than in sumptuously furnished and decorated stone tombs. Of the numerous bodies from all social classes that were mummified in Egypt over a span of more than 2,000 years, only a limited number have survived. Amazingly, many of these are so well preserved that we can observe their individual features, their locks of hair and bits of eyelash and eyebrow, and their still-intact fingernails and toenails.

Other ancient peoples, like the Incas of Peru, also created mummies. But they did so by wrapping the dead in bundles of cloth, grass, and fur, and letting the bodies dry out naturally in

The dry climate of Peru, especially when combined with the cold at higher altitudes, preserved the dead almost as well as the Egyptian embalming process did. This body, with its headdress and necklaces, was found at an ancient Inca grave site.

In 1995, a climbing team discovered the preserved remains of a young Inca girl they named "Juanita." The 500-year-old mummy was apparently a human sacrifice to the mountain gods.

the cold mountain air of the snowy high Andes. Many of the mummified dead in Peru have been found to be children or adolescents. It was a practice of the Incas to sacrifice young people to these mountains, where they believed their gods dwelled. In a solemn religious ceremony, the children would be led to the mountain heights in a drugged state, killed there by a blow to the head, and their bodies left to mummify.

The Aztecs of what is Mexico today also showed their reverence for their gods through the practice of human sacrifice. Among the Aztecs, it was considered an honor to be chosen to have one's living heart cut out and tossed from the top of a pyramid as an offering to the Aztec gods, especially

Huitzilopochtli, the god of the sun and of war. Brave warriors who had already distinguished themselves in battle were the most prized victims.

The Vikings of northern Europe, a seafaring people with a very different background, honored their dead heroes by placing their bodies aboard small seagoing vessels. They then set the ships afire and allowed them to float out to sea.

Finally, there is the example of the emperors of ancient China whose practice it was to have their wives, court officials,

The body of a bearded Viking lord lies strapped to a wooden pallet on a fiery vessel that is being pushed out to sea.

A view of the excavation site outside the city of Xian, Shaanxi Province, in China, where thousands of terra-cotta archers, cavalry troops, charioteers, infantrymen, and horses have gradually been unearthed.

soldiers, and horses buried alive with them in great tombs, for company and protection through eternity.

Happily, this mass smothering of human and animal life ended around 200 B.C. when Emperor Qin Shi Huang decided to be buried instead with an entire life-size army of 8,000 warriors, servants, and horses—all made out of terra-cotta or cast in bronze. Probably Qin (pronounced *Chin* and very likely the origin of the name China) decided that he would feel safer being guarded through eternity by swordsmen who would not soon be reduced to rotting flesh and moldering bones.

3

Funeral Customs:
Among World Religions

Although death rites and customs among the major world religions may vary considerably, they seem to have sprung from a common need. First, some provision must be made for the disposal of the body.

Early peoples employed many different methods, ranging from cannibalism to mummification, from cave burial and water burial to exposure to wildlife and the elements. They also practiced earth burial, entombment, and cremation . . . the customs that are followed by most of the world's religions today.

Second, there is a need at the time of death for a ritual that will provide comfort for the mourners and help to restore balance to their lives after a time of trauma. So, often, there is a funeral or memorial service followed by a specified period of mourning.

Third, most religions also see death as a means of release of the spirit, or soul, of the deceased. This unseen phenomenon is associated with a religious belief in the existence of an afterlife.

Judaism, with a history of more than 5,700 years, is among the oldest religions still practiced today. Judaic law is very specific about the burial of the dead. It calls for an earth burial that must take place as soon as possible after death. Embalming, either by the ancient Egyptian method or in the present-day fashion, is not permitted.

At the time of death, the eyes of the deceased are closed, preferably by a first-born son if he is present. The body is then washed, the nails are trimmed, and the corpse is wrapped in a shroud of fine white linen that must not be too costly. A man's body is also draped in his prayer shawl.

The coffin, too, should be of the simplest type, preferably built of wooden boards, and is kept closed throughout the service. According to ancient law, the body must be allowed to decay quickly and naturally once it is buried. It is also acceptable for an uncoffined body to be placed directly in the ground, a custom that is practiced today in Israel.

The prompt Judaic burial, which probably originated in part for hygienic reasons, is followed by a seven-day mourning period known as the *shiva*. Certain foods, such as eggs and lentils, are recommended for the post-funeral meal because, like the dead, "they have no mouth." Also, their round shapes, having no beginning and no ending, serve as symbols of eternity. It is also the custom among some Jewish people to eat salty foods such as herring directly following a funeral. Such foods are said to replace the tears that have been shed for the deceased.

During the shiva, the immediate family mourners remain at home. They do no work, sit on low stools or even on the floor, and wear cloth slippers instead of shoes. They do not shave or cut their hair. They make a tear or a cut in the clothing worn on the upper part of the body, or they may wear a torn black lapel ribbon. The mirrors in the house are covered so that all vanity is abolished and thoughts are only of the dead.

Friends and neighbors who visit those in mourning during the shiva period may participate in a daily worship service that includes the prayer for the dead.

After seven days, the mourners resume their normal lives. A prayer for the dead should be said daily for the first year and, after that, a prayer is said and a candle is lit each year on the anniversary of the death.

In Judaism the question of the destination of the soul or spirit of the deceased is open to a range of interpretations. The Old Testament makes reference to a place called Sheol, a shadowy netherworld where no differentiation is made between the righteous and the wicked. It is simply the realm of departed spirits, much like the Greek Hades.

There is also a "true" hell in the Old Testament, known as Gehenna, or the Valley of Hinnom. Hinnom is believed to have been a place outside the western wall of Jerusalem where human sacrifices by fire took place. Also called the "valley of slaughter," Hinnom was where the carcasses of animals, the bodies of criminals, and the city's refuse were dumped, and it was presumably the place where the wicked were punished after death.

While most members of the Jewish faith believe that the human spirit, or the soul, lives on after death, its fate is seen differently by Orthodox, Conservative, and Reform branches of the religion. Ultra Orthodox Jews foresee resurrection and reincarnation of the dead with the coming of the Messiah, the long-awaited deliverer of the faithful. At the opposite end of the spectrum are those Jews who feel that the spirit lives on mainly in the inspiration, the good works, and the offspring of the deceased.

Christianity, which grew out of Judaism, has a very distinct belief in the existence of a life of the soul after death. The nature of the Christian afterlife is based on a judgment of the merits of the deceased. The faithful—those who believe in Jesus Christ as Lord and Savior—go to a reward in heaven, while those who have sinned and not repented may be consigned to hell. For some Christians, there is also an intermediate realm known as purgatory, where the evil may be sent for purification.

Rituals, too, vary among the Christian churches such as Roman Catholicism, Eastern Orthodox Catholicism, and the numerous Protestant sects.

For Catholics, if it is at all possible before the advent of death, a priest should administer a last rite called Anointing

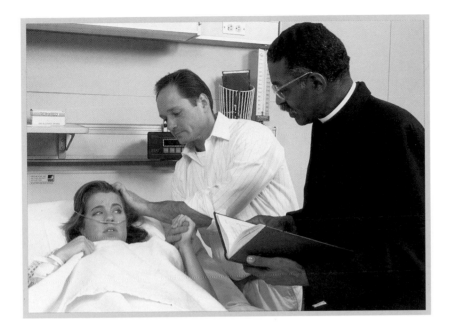

Hospitals and nursing homes are regularly visited by the clergy. A Catholic may request a priest to perform a final rite in the event that death is near.

the Sick. In this ceremony, formerly known as Extreme Unction, the priest blesses the sacramental oil with which he then anoints the forehead and hands of the dying person. He also offers readings from the Scriptures.

Protestants do not follow the practice of receiving a last rite. But both groups tend to observe a vigil, or viewing period, of the dead before burial, lasting usually for two or three days.

This form of display, though, is not required by religious law. Some groups still refer to the viewing, or watching of the body, as a wake. Originally, a wake was an all-night watch beside the corpse that was intended to comfort the spirit of the dead and to protect it from evil. It was also a means of watching to make sure the person was truly dead and would not return to life.

The Christian burial service usually concludes with the transport of the coffin from the funeral parlor or other place of viewing to the church for a mass or other type of religious serv-

A mourner pays respects at an open-coffin funeral in a flower-bedecked Christian chapel.

ice. This is followed by burial in holy ground in a cemetery of the deceased's branch of Christianity. In former times, mourners might wear black for an indefinite period following a death in the family, or would sew black armbands onto their outer garments. Nowadays these outward signs of mourning are seen less often.

In Islam, the religion introduced by the Prophet Mohammed in the seventh century A.D., there are strict rituals to be observed at the time of death. Muslims, as the followers of Islam are known, have burial customs similar to those of Judaism. The deceased's body is washed, wrapped in a seamless white shroud, and must be buried within twenty-four hours if possible. Embalming or other attempts at even short-term preservation are prohibited. A coffin is not required for burial. The body may be placed directly in the ground.

The placement of the body in the grave is a matter of great importance. It must lie with its right side facing Mecca, the holy city in today's Saudi Arabia, where Mohammed was born. Simple prayers may be said at the graveside, and afterward at the mosque or at home. It is the family's duty to repay any debts owed by the deceased, unless they have been forgiven through the mercy of the lenders.

In Islam, as in Christianity, it is believed that souls are judged, and rewarded or punished depending on one's behavior while on earth. In other words, life on earth is seen as a time of testing and preparation for the hereafter. The Islamic versions of heaven and hell are sharply drawn. The souls of Islamic martyrs and other believers whose lives have been unblemished will be transported to a realm of eternal pleasures and delights

This illumination from a 15th-century Turkish manuscript shows the Prophet Mohammed on a tour of the infernal regions. He encounters souls in chains and shackles, condemned for hypocrisy and flattery.

35

called paradise. Sinners and unbelievers will be sent to a place of intense heat and dense smoke known as Jihanna, which quite clearly seems to derive from the Gehenna, or Valley of Hinnom, of the Old Testament.

In all three of these faiths—Judaism, Christianity, and Islam—suicide is considered a sin, based on the belief that it is God who determines when one's life shall end. During the Middle Ages in Europe, those who took their own lives were linked with murderers and could not be buried in churchyards or in other sanctified ground. Often, suicides and criminals were buried at a crossroads on the theory that their spirits would be confused by the movement of passing wagons and foot traffic, and would forever be unable to rest.

Yet, there have been Christian cultist groups that have committed mass suicide in the belief that they would be rewarded by God with a better life. One shattering example was that of the People's Temple under the leadership of a man named Jim Jones. Jones set up a religious commune in a place he called Jonestown, in Guyana, on the northern coast of South America. In November 1978, he convinced his followers, most of them American families with children, to drink cyanide-laced Kool-Aid, promising that through their deaths they would gain immediate entrance to the kingdom of heaven. More than 900 people—276 of them children—were found dead in the Guyanese jungle.

Other world religions have taken a different view of suicide. In Hinduism, which has a very long history in India, it was considered the duty of a man's widow to throw herself on his funeral pyre to be burned alive. This act, which is called suttee,

In 1978, when officials visited Jonestown in Guyana to investigate charges that people were held against their will, cult members killed U.S. Representative Leo J. Ryan and a number of others. Shortly afterward, Jim Jones ordered the members of his cult to commit mass suicide, resulting in the horrifying event known as the Jonestown Massacre.

An 18th-century engraving shows a scene from the islands off Indonesia in which a wife has chosen to be buried with her deceased husband.

was meant to show a wife's complete devotion to her husband. It also served to dispose of a woman who might become a burden on society. The British, who at one time ruled India, officially banned this practice in 1828. But it continued in secret among the devout for some years.

Hinduism decrees that the body of the deceased must be burned rather than buried, as in Judaism, Christianity, and Islam, because it is believed that only immolation, or burning, can release the human soul from the body. The destiny of the individual's soul is to pass from body to body until it becomes totally pure. So each person must live through many reincarnations, sometimes as a human, sometimes as an animal, in striving toward this goal. Only through this process can the

38

soul eventually be liberated from the cycles of life and death, and be united with Brahman, the Hindu supreme god.

According to Hindu law, cremation must follow swiftly after death. In India, a densely populated country with a predominantly hot climate, this also serves as a public health measure. The body is wrapped in a shroud and placed on a funeral pyre built of twigs and other kindling wood. Sandalwood may be added to the pyre for its fragrant odor and also for its oily content, which helps the pyre to burn more rapidly. Another substance, ghee, which is clarified butter, is often added as well for this reason. The eldest son or grandson of the deceased is delegated to light the pyre.

Landings along the banks of India's holy Ganges River, which are known as ghats, are the scene of many cremations. These ceremonies are performed in keeping with the belief that by offering the body to the Hindu god of fire, the corrupt soul will be purified and eventually released. After the cremation, the ashes of the deceased are collected and deposited in the river. The Ganges is said to carry more human ashes than any other river on earth.

Buddhism, a religion that is widely practiced in central and eastern Asia, grew out of the teachings of its founder, known as Gautama Buddha, who lived about five hundred years before Christ. The goal of Buddhism is a state of enlightenment and complete peace of the soul, known as nirvana.

To achieve nirvana, one must learn the path of righteous living. As in the Hindu faith, the soul approaches its ideal state through the cycle of death and reincarnation. So, like the Hindus, most Buddhists are cremated. The funeral pyre is usually sprinkled with holy oil, and the cremations are accompanied by chanting and the beating of gongs. The ashes of the deceased are then either scattered, buried, or placed in an urn for the family to keep.

The ashes from funeral pyres are swept into the Ganges River, in which many devout Hindus also bathe.

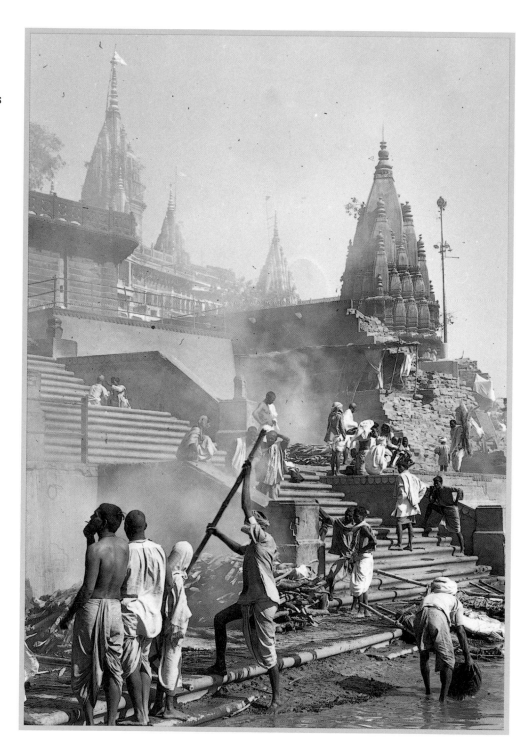

In countries like India, China, and Japan, there are many offshoots of Hinduism and Buddhism that follow similar funeral practices. The religion of the Sikhs of northwest India is a blend of Hinduism and Buddhism. The Jains, another religious group of India, also believe that the soul may inhabit many different bodies, and they take extreme precautions not to kill even the tiniest insect.

In China the practices of Confucianism and Taoism are sometimes followed along with Buddhism. But actually these two belief systems are more involved with ethical behavior and virtuous thinking than with strictly religious ritual.

In both China and Japan, there is a history of cultural and religious approval of suicide. Warriors who had failed in their mission, ministers who fell out of favor with the emperor or other ruling power, and those who found themselves personally disgraced were virtually required to perform an act of self-inflicted death. In Japan, hara-kiri, also known as seppuku, was the time-honored method. Using a dagger, the would-be suicide

The body of a young Buddhist monk is cremated near Seoul, South Korea.

accomplished disembowelment by making a deep cut across the abdomen, followed by an upward thrust toward the heart.

As recently as World War II, this ritual was performed by members of the Japanese military who refused to surrender. And during the war, over 3,900 Japanese kamikaze pilots chose suicide by crashing their bomb-laden planes directly into enemy targets. Since World War II, ceremonial hara-kiri has diminished considerably in Japan. But shamed government officials and others in public life, caught in corruption and similar scandals, may well seek a less flamboyant means of exiting the scene.

Japan's oldest religion is known as Shintoism. Followers of Shinto worshiped many gods, including nature deities, heroes of the past, and even the emperor, who was at one time declared to be divine. The Shinto religion originally dictated that the dead must be buried in the earth. But the influence of Buddhism, and the shortage of land in Japan, have led to the general practice of cremating the dead. The remains are then either buried or kept in an urn or other container by the family.

4

Funeral Customs:
Death in America,
Then and Now

Among the colonists and frontier folk of early America, death was an all-too-common occurrence. It visited infants, toddlers, and older children, young mothers, and many other adults in the prime years of life. In fact, death was so expected in the simple homesteads on the new continent that preparations for it were always kept on hand.

Almost no household was without a supply of lumber for making a coffin and a handwoven winding sheet to shroud the body of the next to die. Wedding gowns, too, were often used as burial garments for wives who died in childbirth or as a result of extreme physical toil.

Funerals in those early days were conducted by family members with the help of neighbors. Almost no professional undertakers existed. Relatives or friends washed, laid out, and dressed the body. The wake, or watch, for family and visitors was held in the parlor if there was one, or simply the "best" room of the house.

Women in colonial times led hard lives. Children often did not live past infancy.
This 1772 painting, Rachel Weeping, by Charles W. Peale, shows a mother mourning the loss of her child to smallpox.

Afterward the coffin would be carried on foot to the meetinghouse or church, if it was not too far away, for a religious service, and then to the burying ground. More often, in the rural New England communities, it was taken directly to the family graveyard.

The European ancestors of the American colonists had been known to bury their dead under the floors of old stone churches or in vaults in the church walls. But in the raw wilderness of early America, no such buildings existed, so earth burial became the universal custom.

Among the poorer colonial families, no extended mourning period was observed, except as a private matter, for all mourners had to return immediately to their everyday chores. Prosperous colonists, though, like the Dutch residents of early New York, held more formal funerals and observances.

New Amsterdam Dutch families invited people to funerals by sending out messengers known as *aanspreeckers*, men dressed in black and wearing black crepe mourning ribbons on their hats. At the funeral it was customary to serve Madeira wine and to distribute thick round cookies flavored with caraway seeds that were known as *doed-koecks*. They were marked with the initials of the deceased and would be taken home and saved for years as a memento, in the same way that sample pieces of wedding cake are kept.

The colonists known as the Pennsylvania Dutch, who were really of German origin, served post-funeral feasts to replenish the energies of family members and neighbors who had driven a long distance. The guests might be treated to boiled smoked hams and stewed chickens, accompanied by the traditional "seven sweets and seven sours"—an array of fruit preserves and jellies balanced by pickles and relishes. And no Pennsylvania German burial feast could end without a serving of raisin pie, which was commonly known as funeral pie.

Similarly, in the colonial South, the well-to-do plantation owners renewed the spirits of the mourners with rum punch and cakes, and often with heartier fare.

By the early 1800s, funerals in the United States were becoming more commercial. Carpenters were providing coffins, either built to order or ready-made, and carriage makers were designing special funeral coaches decorated with black draperies and drawn by a team of shiny black horses.

Black was viewed as the color of death in most Western countries. The ancient Romans, and other cultures before them, believed that a person wearing black would not be recognized by the ghost of the deceased. But most mourners who have worn black have probably thought of it simply as a fitting symbol of grief. Yet in Eastern countries like China, white is the traditional color of mourning.

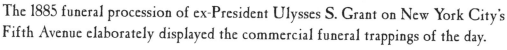
The 1885 funeral procession of ex-President Ulysses S. Grant on New York City's Fifth Avenue elaborately displayed the commercial funeral trappings of the day.

During the second half of the 1800s, funerals in America grew increasingly formal and elaborate. Black-bordered funeral invitations were sent out, and house doors were hung with black wreaths and mourning ribbons. It became the custom to distribute memorial tokens to the funeral guests. Often they took the form of lockets, brooches, bracelets, rings, or watch fobs, either made from or containing samples of the hair of the deceased.

Nineteenth-century memorial tokens

Shops stocked special black funeral cloth by the yard for widows and other family members who went into mourning for a year or more. There were even black-bordered handkerchiefs and writing paper to be had. And for servants or others who didn't dress in full mourning garb, there were black armbands that were sewn onto the left sleeves of garments just above the elbow.

The fashion for the long-term display of grief in the late 1800s was patterned in part on the behavior of Queen Victoria of England. When her husband, Prince Albert, died in 1861, the queen withdrew from social activities and dressed in black until her death forty years later, in 1901.

In the United States, the Civil War gave rise to the practice of embalming those who fell in battle so that their bodies could be preserved long enough to be shipped home. This method of partial preservation allowed funerals to become ever more lavish. Bodies could remain on view for several days if necessary, and important persons like kings and presidents could lie in state for an extended period.

Following the assassination of Abraham Lincoln in April 1865, the president's embalmed body was placed aboard a funeral train that traveled slowly for fourteen days, covering the 1,700 miles (2,737 kilometers) from Washington, D.C., to Springfield, Illinois, where he was buried. At each stop, the coffin was removed from the train and opened so that some of

Queen Victoria

The embalming process developed during the Civil War allowed the public viewing of President Abraham Lincoln's body, shown here in New York City. A train carried the body most of the way from Washington to Illinois, where Lincoln was buried.

the many thousands who waited along the route could view the president. Refrigeration was used to prolong the preservation of Lincoln's body.

Widespread embalming, of the kind practiced in ancient Egypt, had ceased to exist by the early Christian era. But through the centuries that followed, various methods were used to embalm royal persons, battle heroes, and saints. Many such attempts were only partially successful, and often the "preserved" bodies were suspected of being little more than wax images.

The "father" of modern embalming in the United States was a failed medical student by the name of Thomas Holmes. Having worked on cadavers in medical school, Holmes began in the 1860s to offer his services to the families of those who had died on the Civil War battlefields, charging one hundred dollars per body. His method was to remove the blood and other bodily fluids that would cause rapid decay and to introduce a formaldehyde-type embalming fluid in their place. Thus the decomposition that might begin within twenty-four hours could be put off for several days, allowing for shipment home by railroad or even by horse and wagon.

Although Holmes's embalming skills did not approach those of the ancient Egyptians in terms of truly long-term preservation, he became a rich man and his methods were to be widely adopted by the funeral directors of the century that followed.

Funerals in the United States became big business in the 1900s. The plain wooden coffin of earlier times gave way to the much more costly solid mahogany, satin-lined casket, or even the metal casket of copper- or lead-coated steel.

Funeral directors began to offer burial vaults as well. Constructed of concrete, metal, asphalt, or fiberglass, the burial vault was meant to enclose the casket and to prevent the grave site from sinking once the wooden coffin beneath the ground began to disintegrate. Like the metal coffin, the burial vault was also designed to afford "greater protection" for the deceased.

Other costly services and furnishings came to be offered in the 1900s. They included embalming and makeup, fashionable "death finery" clothing, and a tastefully decorated "slumber room" in which family and friends might view the deceased before burial or even cremation.

Understandably, many families continue to be drawn to making large death and burial expenditures for a variety of reasons. They may feel obliged to do so through love, loyalty, or respect for the deceased. Or they may simply regard a costly funeral as fitting because it is customary or because it is a status symbol.

But how long does the padded satin lining of the most costly coffin endure, and what happens to the embalmed body itself?

After only a couple of months, the body dug up from the grave will be covered with mold. The luxurious casket lining will be stained with body fluids, and the polished wooden exterior will have begun to disintegrate.

A sealed metal coffin will, of course, hold up better. But the corpse inside it will suffer horrible consequences as the putrefaction bacteria go to work in an oxygen-starved atmosphere. It is, in fact, preferable for the body to decay as rapidly as possible through direct contact with the soil, enclosed in no more than a coffin of boards or only a body shroud.

Although there are no religious or state laws in America that require embalming (except in the case of a body shipped by air, rail, or other common carrier), over 65 percent of American funerals continue to be "open casket," and most of the bodies on view are embalmed.

In addition to pumping 3 to 6 gallons (11 to 23 liters) of embalming fluid into the body of the deceased, the embalmer firms, sets, and makes up the face, hands, and other visible features of the body. Surgical thread or holding pins may be used to give the mouth and lips a relaxed, lifelike expression. The hair will have been shampooed and the fingernails manicured. A male corpse will be shaved, and a female may have the hair styled and the fingernails polished.

Even murder and accident victims can have their facial features restored by means of liquid injection, cotton padding, patching with tinted wax, and the application of cosmetics.

Such an attempt was made on the face of President John F. Kennedy, who was assassinated by gunshot wounds to the head in November 1963. Kennedy's skull, however, had been severely damaged, and the waxy restoration of his features was extremely artificial-looking. As a result, Mrs. Kennedy ordered that the president's coffin remain closed during the time he lay in state.

The funerals of prominent political figures and other famous persons have always drawn large numbers of public mourners. In 1865, on the occasion of Abraham Lincoln's death, families drove for miles or walked long distances simply to line the railroad tracks for a glimpse of the slow-moving funeral train that bore the president's body back to Illinois from the nation's capital.

Millions of saddened citizens were said to have gathered at the various stops along the route in order to file past the open coffin and view the president's face for the last time.

Some public figures, however, have looked with distaste on having an open coffin at a state funeral. Before President Franklin Delano Roosevelt died in 1945, he left instructions that his body was not to be embalmed and that his coffin was to remain closed. The president also specified a coffin of plain dark wood, and he requested that it be carried on a caisson, a two-wheeled horse-drawn gun carriage, rather than in a hearse.

Unfortunately, Roosevelt's instructions were locked away in a safe and were not found until after his funeral had taken place. As a result, his body was embalmed, it was placed in a costly metal coffin, and the coffin was transported in a motorized hearse. But the president's main request—for a closed coffin—was honored because he and Mrs. Roosevelt had often discussed the fact that they both disliked the practice of exhibiting a corpse to the public at a state funeral.

Following the shock of the assassination of John F. Kennedy in Dallas on November 22, 1963, the president's body was flown back to Washington, D.C. It was decided that the funeral arrangements should be modeled on those of President Abraham Lincoln. Therefore, Kennedy's body, in its flag-draped coffin, which remained closed, lay in state in the Capitol Rotunda while thousands, including many foreign dignitaries, filed past the casket. The viewing line for the mourning public was three miles (4.75 kilometers) long. The casket was then transported to St. Matthew's Cathedral in Washington on a caisson. President Kennedy was buried in Arlington National Cemetery.

While it is frequently argued that embalming is a sanitary measure, the process as practiced today does not dry out the soft tissues of the body, where many serious disease organisms are found. A more effective means of ensuring against the spread of disease would be either a prompt burial or cremation.

While the ancient Greeks and Romans burned the bodies of the dead, as did Hindus and Buddhists through the centuries,

A caisson bears the flag-draped coffin of President John F. Kennedy. At Arlington National Cemetery, Mrs. Kennedy lit an eternal flame to burn atop the president's grave.

modern Western peoples have been slow to adopt this method of disposing of the dead. In England, cremation became legal in 1884, and in 1885 three bodies were reported to have been cremated.

Today, however, more than 75 percent of Britons accept cremation as both sanitary and practical. Cremation is even more widely practiced in modern Japan, where land is so extremely limited that if the bodies of the dead were buried they would virtually crowd out the living.

In the United States, it is estimated that only 30 percent of the deceased are cremated. But this figure is increasing steadily, with most cremations taking place on the East and West coasts.

A columbarium at Rosedale Cemetery in New Jersey displays urns of cremated remains in marble niches. The niches can be fitted with glass front windows if desired. Outside the columbarium is an Urn Garden, especially designed for cremation burials.

The first American crematorium was built in Pennsylvania in 1876. Since then, religious objections to cremation have relaxed considerably. The Roman Catholic Church has accepted cremation since 1963, as do most Protestant groups. Orthodox Judaism, however, does not.

In the modern crematorium, an average adult body is reduced to 4 to 10 pounds (2 to 4.5 kilograms) of bone fragments, depending on the skeletal structure of the deceased. The process, which takes place at a temperature of 1,600 to 2,000 degrees Fahrenheit (871 to 1,093 degrees Celsius) is completed within two to three hours. The bone fragments, which make up the remains, may then be pulverized into finer particles for scattering. Morticians often refer to them as "cremains."

Cremated remains may also be placed in an urn or other receptacle for keeping, either at home or in a niche in a structure made up of tiny vaults, known as a columbarium. Many cemeteries allow cremated remains to be buried, and funeral directors provide miniature caskets for this purpose.

Bodies entering the cremation chamber do not need to have been embalmed or otherwise prepared, except for the removal of mechanical devices such as pacemakers or defibrillators. These battery-operated devices, which are implanted in the body to regulate life-threatening irregularities in the heart rhythm, will explode when subjected to the extreme heat of the cremation process. The body itself need not be enclosed in anything but a simple, inexpensive, combustible box, which is destroyed in the cremation process.

A direct cremation should cost only a few hundred dollars as compared with a full-scale, open-casket funeral, the cost of which may run into many thousands of dollars. If, however, a family selects an expensive casket and an embalming procedure for the purpose of having a viewing prior to cremation, the cost will be considerably more.

The urn as pop art: the ashes are in the small bottle being held up by a hand.

55

Cremation is frequently performed directly and privately, and it is often followed by a memorial service at which the remains of the deceased are not present.

For those who do not favor either burial or cremation, there is a third choice—the donation of the body to a medical school or teaching hospital for anatomical research. Like the contribution of organs to benefit the living, many people feel that this is the best purpose to which the body of the deceased can be put. But, of course, much depends on personal feelings and religious convictions.

Finally, for those who still cling to the prospect of physical immortality, there is the scientifically far-fetched but oft-discussed idea of having one's body frozen at the time of death and stored until a cure can be found for the disease that caused it.

This process, known as cryonics or cryogenics, first drew attention in the 1960s. It involves draining the blood from the body and injecting a fluid to retard damage to the cells. The "temporarily deceased" is then wrapped and stored in a capsule that is maintained at an extremely low temperature with liquid nitrogen. Thus the "patient" in cryonic suspension awaits resuscitation when a cure is developed for the disease that had proved fatal.

For many years following the death of Walt Disney in 1966, rumors persisted that the Hollywood mogul of animated cartoons had had his body frozen. Disney had been a smoker all his life, and he died of cancer that had originated in his lungs and spread throughout his body. Although the sixty-five-year-old Disney had always had an exceptionally morbid attitude toward death, he knew better than to believe that his diseased organs could be reborn. Disney's corpse was cremated, and his ashes buried in Forest Lawn Cemetery in Glendale, California.

Though the cryogenic freezing of tissues such as skin, eye corneas, and blood for later surgical use has proven to be very effective, no one has yet established the validity of freezing an entire human corpse with the idea of curing and reawakening it at a later date.

One of the reasons that so many believed Disney had chosen the cryonic route to possible resuscitation was his strong control of the Disney enterprises. His codirectors were said to have actually feared that Disney would one day come back and "get even" with all those who had taken his plans for the company in a direction that he did not approve.

Cryonics does serve as a valuable means of storing blood and tissue, including human eggs and sperm for artificial insemination. But cryonicists today are still highly doubtful that even a relatively "healthy" corpse could be reanimated because the freezing process itself results in the rupture of many cellular membranes. They theorize that reanimation might have a chance of success if freezing the body took place before death. But such a procedure could well involve a commercial cryonics firm in a charge of murder.

At the present time there are said to be about two dozen persons and also a number of pets being held in frozen suspension in the United States. The cost of initiating and maintaining the cryonics process for an individual begins in the hundreds of thousands of dollars and may well run into millions. Should the maintenance costs stop being paid or should the cryonics firm go bankrupt, the frozen bodies will thaw out and go the way of all flesh. For those pioneers, though, who are attempting the cryonics route to immortality, the motto truly is "Never say die!"

5

Final Resting Places: Graveyards and How They Grew

From earliest times, the disposal of the dead has taken many forms. But it is earth burial that provides a major source of information about the final resting places of our forebears.

As soon as prehistoric humans settled into farming communities, they began to provide large permanent burial places for their dead. The graveyards of the Neolithic, or New Stone Age, peoples often took the form of burial mounds—artificial hillocks of earth and stone constructed over a mass grave. Such mounds have been found in many parts of Europe, in Japan, and in North America.

In England these prehistoric burial mounds are called barrows, or, if covered only with heaps of stones, they are known as cairns. One of the largest barrows, Silbury Hill in Wiltshire, is 130 feet (40 meters) high, and covers 5 acres (2 hectares).

Germany, too, has mounds of great size, so large in fact that they were once believed to be the graves of a race of giants. Other prehistoric burial mounds have been found in northern France, Spain, Portugal, and Russia. Those found in Japan are sometimes constructed in the shape of a keyhole rather than a circle, and appear to have been the grave sites of emperors and members of the court rather than of the farmers and villagers of the early settlements.

The best-known burial mounds in North America are those in southern Ohio, where an early Native American people appear to have formed a stable and sizeable agricultural community. These extensive earthworks reveal that some of the dead were buried while others were first cremated. But what makes these Native American mounds so significant are the many artifacts that were interred with the dead—carved stone pipes in animal shapes, stone tools and weapons, pottery, and numerous objects made from copper, mica, shell, and even grizzly-bear teeth.

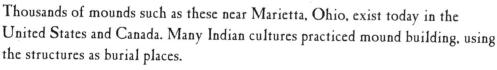

Thousands of mounds such as these near Marietta, Ohio, exist today in the United States and Canada. Many Indian cultures practiced mound building, using the structures as burial places.

Among burial sites from ancient times, one of the most accessible is the catacombs of Rome during the early Christian era. From about A.D. 200, the persecuted members of the new religion hid in the corridors and recessed rooms of the city's underground cemetery, which had been carved out of soft volcanic rock. Soon this subterranean world became the scene of Christian grave sites. To this day, one can walk through the passageways of the Roman catacombs, lined with the skeletal remains of Christians and others who needed to hide from the authorities.

After Christianity came to be accepted in the Roman Empire, during the latter part of the fourth century, it became safe to abandon the secret burial sites, and the dead were interred in graveyards surrounding the newly built churches. One could also be buried in the church building itself, although such honors were usually reserved for prominent members of the clergy and other dignitaries. The great stone churches and cathedrals of the European Middle Ages offered underground crypts for the dead and even burials just beneath the church floor.

But neither churches nor their graveyards could begin to accommodate the dead in the event of a plague or other natural disaster, or a war. Among the worse epidemics to ravage Europe was the bubonic plague between 1347 and 1350, known as the Black Death. It took its name from the dark-blood, egg-size swellings, or buboes, that appeared in the neck, armpits, and groin of the victims of the disease, and which almost always preceded death.

The plague was transmitted from the Middle East to Europe by sailing ships that carried infected rats, and was spread by fleas that lived off the rats. It began in the Black Sea and Mediterranean ports, and reached northern Europe and England, killing 25 million people, one third of the population of Europe at the time.

A 14th-century painting shows the agony of plague victims in the town of Basel in Switzerland.

In his classic work, the *Decameron*, the Italian writer Giovanni Boccaccio told about a group of men and women who fled the plague-infested city of Florence for the country. He also described the plague conditions in Florence. Each morning the corpses would be dragged out of their homes, piled up at their front doors, and carried away on ordinary wooden boards to be buried in huge trenches outside the city, layer upon layer, until the trench was filled to the top and a new one had to be dug. All too often, Boccaccio wrote, the dead "were so sparsely covered with earth that the dogs dragged them out and devoured their bodies."

As populations grew all over the world, whether there were mass deaths or not, burial grounds became increasingly crowded. Churchyards and other cemeteries in Europe were so heaped with bodies that it often became necessary to remove

A crowded old cemetery in Prague, Czech Republic, is ringed by the city's vigorous growth.

63

Père Lachaise was
built outside of Paris
to alleviate the city's
overcrowded cemetery
problem.

skeletal and even partially decayed remains in order to make room for new grave sites. And burial pits, into which lime was scattered for rapid deterioration of the body, were in common use for the poor and for criminals.

In Paris the situation was so strained by the 1700s that the authorities arranged for the construction of the huge rural cemetery of Père Lachaise. Père Lachaise was opened in 1804 and houses the graves of such notables of France as the composer Chopin and the playwright Molière, as well as the popular American singer Jim Morrison of The Doors. Chopin, however, who was of Polish birth, had his heart removed before interment so that it might be entombed in the wall of a church in Warsaw, the capital of his native land.

Even in the wide open spaces of America, it was inevitable that the family burying ground and the village churchyard would become congested, as the population increased, with the ever-growing numbers of the dead.

In coastal and eastern cities like New York, Boston, and Philadelphia, which became home to waves of European immigrants starting in the 1830s, more and more land was required to serve the living. In 1832, New York City's borough of Manhattan experienced a horrifying pileup of corpses when it was struck by a cholera epidemic, caused by the drinking of contaminated well water.

The only way to increase burial space on the narrow island of Manhattan had been to bury the dead atop one another, as many as three deep. As in European cities, heavy rains exposed the corpses in various stages of decay, and attracted roving animals, bringing on a serious sanitation problem.

The highly personal concept of burial in the village churchyard among family and friends, so popular in New England from colonial days until the early 1800s, abruptly stopped as swelling population left no more vacancies.

By the time a second cholera epidemic hit, in 1849, the city had opened new burying grounds across the river in the less-populous borough of Queens. Horse-drawn wagons, loaded with human remains, were ferried, often by night, to the new graveyards in western Queens, which soon became known as the city's Cemetery Belt. Some of the remains were skeletons dug up from Manhattan's graveyards to make way for business and housing districts. Others were the newly dead who had fallen victim to yellow fever or cholera epidemics, or other common causes of mortality at the time.

By the early 1800s other cities, too, were forced to seek out new burying grounds. But rather than hastily interring both recent and earlier remains, often in mass graves as in the early Queens cemeteries, the city fathers planned out suburban parklands that came to be known as garden cemeteries.

The first among these was Mount Auburn Cemetery in Cambridge, Massachusetts, just outside Boston. Founded in 1831, Mount Auburn became a sprawling, well-manicured greensward dotted with lush plantings and small ponds. People came for afternoon strolls as well as to admire the growing

This view of the handsomely designed tomb of Mary Baker Eddy, the founder of Christian Science, shows the natural beauty at Cambridge's Mount Auburn Cemetery.

66

number of handsome grave sites and monuments, some featuring Egyptian obelisks and Greek columns.

Among the famous buried at Mount Auburn are Christian Science founder Mary Baker Eddy; writer and physician Oliver Wendell Holmes; poet Henry Wadsworth Longfellow; and artist Winslow Homer.

Another park for the living as well as the dead was suburban Philadelphia's Laurel Hill Cemetery, founded in 1836. Here, too, were winding paths, stands of trees, meadows, and brooks. Laurel Hill and other garden cemeteries were enclosed with high gates. Visiting hours were thus controlled. No food or dogs or unaccompanied children might enter and, unlike the old open graveyards, the dead were protected from grave robbers. As a result, more elaborate memorials and funeral monuments were erected in the garden cemeteries.

*N*ot to be outdone, New York City, too, developed garden cemeteries that were to become famous for the illustrious names buried within and the lavishness of their memorials. The first of these was Green-Wood Cemetery in Brooklyn, which opened in the late 1830s, fifty years before the Brooklyn Bridge—connecting Brooklyn and Manhattan—was built across the East River.

Due to the river's fast-moving currents, crossings by barge were hazardous to the horse-drawn carriages carrying coffins and mourners. Unexpected water burials were not uncommon, as coffins slid from their hearses before reaching the opposite shore.

Nonetheless, Green-Wood Cemetery was *the* place to be buried in the 1860s and 1870s, when it became the final resting place of the founders of *The New York Times*, the *New York Herald*, and of Horace Greeley, founder and editor of the *New York Tribune*. Greeley was also well known for his support of the

An 1899 Decoration Day (now known as Memorial Day) photograph shows Green-Wood Cemetery as the place to be for the socially prominent living as well as the dead.

homesteading movement and for his oft-repeated words of advice: "Go west, young man. Go west." To Greeley's eternal embarrassment, the sculpted figure of his upper body that surmounts his tombstone faces due east.

Other famous persons buried at Green-Wood include inventors Elias Howe and Samuel F. B. Morse, jeweler Charles Lewis Tiffany, piano manufacturer Charles Steinway, and even such disreputable characters as criminal Albert Anastasia and gangster Joey Gallo. Among the cemetery's most flamboyant monuments is that of Brooklyn's seltzer king, John Matthews. It won an 1870 funerary art prize for its profusion of sculpted stone gargoyles, as well as bears, squirrels, and other forest animals.

Another final resting place of renown is New York City's Woodlawn Cemetery in the Bronx, which opened in 1863 to relieve the flow of Manhattan funeral traffic that was crowding the docks, seeking to get to Brooklyn's Green-Wood Cemetery.

Soon Woodlawn became an extraordinary memorial site of rolling landscapes shaded by many trees. And here, the rich and the famous from the fields of finance, government, science, journalism, the arts, and entertainment left their grave markers and mausoleums. When F. W. Woolworth, the millionaire who had created the five-and-ten-cents store, died in 1919, he chose to be buried like an Egyptian pharaoh in a sphinx-guarded, aboveground stone tomb, decorated with ancient Egyptian columns and motifs.

Not surprisingly, New York's beloved mayor from 1933 to 1945, Fiorello H. La Guardia, is buried at Woodlawn Cemetery. But much less expectedly, so is Bat Masterson, the famed Buffalo hunter, gold prospector, and frontier sheriff of Dodge City, Kansas, in its "Wild West" days. Masterson actually moved to New York City at the age of forty-eight. He became a sports editor for the *Morning Telegraph* and died there in 1921 while working at his desk.

Herman Melville's gravestone

One of the strangest tombstones at Woodlawn Cemetery is that of author Herman Melville, who died in 1891. The main feature of Melville's grave monument is a large scroll carved out of stone and left completely blank. The mystery of why the scroll does not contain the titles of some of Melville's many books, and especially his masterpiece, *Moby Dick*, has never been satisfactorily explained. One answer may be that at the time of Melville's death his popularity as a writer was at low ebb.

Melville himself was said to have designed the blank scroll. Perhaps he was trying to say how meaningless a life devoted to writing could be. He was never to know that his work would be rediscovered in the 1920s and that *Moby Dick*, which had been published in 1851, would come to be considered a classic.

The 1900s were to see a new concept in final resting places, far different from the village graveyards of the 1700s, and even from the garden cemeteries of the 1800s. This new concept began to take shape as early as 1917 when a burial-plot salesman by the name of Hubert Eaton found himself manager of a scraggly, run-down cemetery in Glendale, California, known as Forest Lawn.

Eaton, a minister's son from Missouri, was originally a mining engineer who had gone west to operate a gold mine in Nevada. When the mine failed, Eaton turned to other endeavors.

At Forest Lawn, Eaton began to envision a new kind of cemetery, a vast memorial park offering every possible kind of service and facility for the deceased, as well as numerous attractions for the living. He saw a combination theme park and one-stop shopping center for funerals.

Eaton dreamed of entry gates wider and higher than those at Buckingham Palace, marble statuary ranging from a procession of baby ducks to a reproduction of Michelangelo's *David*,

Forest Lawn held its first Easter sunrise service in 1923. This aerial view of the traditional service shows just a small portion of the cemetery's grounds as it grew to vast proportions.

churches and chapels radiant with stained-glass windows, a museum, a gift shop, flower shops, a casket-selection emporium, a mortuary building with over twenty slumber rooms, a wide choice of resting places in both belowground graves and aboveground mausoleums, and even a columbarium for the remains of those who had chosen cremation.

Hubert Eaton's dream came true. By 1961, Forest Lawn was home to over 200,000, and more than 6,500 a year were "dying to get in." Today, in fact, there are five Forest Lawns. Four of them, also in southern California, are replicas of the original Forest Lawn Memorial Park in Glendale, where Hubert Eaton himself was buried when he died a multimillionaire in 1966 at the age of eighty-five.

As might be expected, a roll call of those who rest at Forest Lawn reads like a history of the Hollywood movie industry. A tiny sampling includes such celebrities of the early and mid-1900s, as Humphrey Bogart, Errol Flynn, Walt Disney, W. C. Fields, Clark Gable, Carole Lombard, Mary Pickford, George Raft, Will Rogers, and Spencer Tracy.

But the resting places of Hollywood's famous names aren't the only reason the living are drawn to Forest Lawn. They come to see the huge religious paintings, to admire the gem collection in the museum, to buy postcards and pottery souvenirs decorated with views of the cemetery, and—yes—to be married in the wedding chapels of Forest Lawn.

*M*ore grandiose even than burial in a great memorial park would be to have a freestanding tomb of one's own, surrounded possibly by a private parkland or similar domain. The first such tombs that come to mind are the great pyramids of the ancient Egyptian pharaohs. Or we can fast-forward to India's Taj Mahal, built in 1631 by the Muslim emperor Shah

Jahan for his favorite wife, who died giving birth to their four-teenth child.

Lenin's tomb in Moscow is yet another example of a free-standing mausoleum. Its sole occupant is Russia's revolutionary leader who died in 1924, his specially embalmed body preserved to waxlike perfection and sealed in glass.

The United States, too, has its heroes' tombs, the best known probably being the Tomb of the Unknown Soldier at Arlington National Cemetery in Virginia, Abraham Lincoln's tomb in Springfield, Illinois, and Ulysses S. Grant's tomb in New York City.

The tombs of Lincoln and Grant reflect the taste of the latter half of the 1800s for monuments that borrow architectural features from ancient times. Lincoln's tomb, which is topped with an Egyptian-inspired obelisk, houses the remains of Lincoln, his wife, and three of their sons. Since its dedication in 1874, it has had to be reconstructed twice because of the damage done by souvenir hunters eager to chip away at its stones and its bronze statuary.

Although President Ulysses S. Grant's second term in office was plagued with scandal, and he died in financially reduced circumstances, a committee was formed to raise money for a tomb deemed suitable for the man who had also been commanding general of the Union forces during the Civil War.

It was decided that Grant's mausoleum should be a columned square building with a columned round dome, derived from the design of the classical temples of ancient Greece and Rome. It took twelve years—from Grant's death in 1885 to the dedication of the tomb in 1897—for his body to be placed in his mausoleum in New York City's Riverside Park. During that time, Grant's remains were kept in a steel casket in a redbrick vault near the building site. When Grant's wife died in 1902, her body was placed alongside his in the tomb.

Ulysses S. Grant's tomb

73

While some may rest in spacious surroundings into the unforeseeable future, others are given only a limited time in the grave. This is especially true in places where cremation is frowned upon and land resources are very scarce. One example is the Italian city of Venice, which is made up of tiny islands in a lagoon.

To be buried on the Venetian cemetery island of San Michele, bodies are ferried by floating hearse across the lagoon, but are interred only for a limited period of twelve years. Once that time has elapsed, the bones are dug up and placed in an ossuary, a communal storehouse also known as a boneyard, in order to make room for new burials. Many other Italian cities such as Sorrento, which has a very hilly terrain, also follow this practice.

Another option is aboveground entombment such as takes place in New Orleans and other very low-lying places in the United States and elsewhere. Because of the high groundwater level in the Mississippi Delta, a freshly dug grave will quickly fill up with water. So bodies are placed in vaults or crypts in aboveground depositories. Space in some of these depositories, however, can only be obtained on a rental basis. If the rent is not paid, the crypt will be opened, the remains will be "evicted," and the space rented to a new occupant.

The shortage of land available for burial has also led to the creation of high-rise structures such as the five-story circular tower that was built in Milan, Italy, in 1969, containing crypts for more than three thousand bodies. Nashville, Tennessee, not to be outdone, created its own twenty-story mausoleum, shaped like a huge cross and dubbed "The Death Hilton." Similarly, Rio de Janeiro, the Brazilian city, squeezed between the mountains and the sea, put up a thirty-nine-story high-rise mausoleum in 1972. A grandiose structure of glass and concrete, it was to become known as "The Big Condominium in the Sky."

Cemeteries look like miniature cities in New Orleans, where in-ground burial would mean being consigned to a watery grave.

This Hollywood Cemetery mausoleum features five tiers of burial crypts and a vaulted glass ceiling.

Most popular today in cemeteries in the United States are mausoleums of one or two storeys, each level lined with crypts into which coffins can be slid, five to seven tiers of crypts per floor. The new mausoleums provide elevators for visitors, and are advertised as being "light and airy" and "in a park-like setting." They are designed to be comforting to prospective buyers who do not like the thought of lying beneath the soil, as well as to family members who may be enticed by the indoor amenities of stained-glass windows and chandeliers.

Mausoleum crypts are usually sold on a pre-need basis, like choice burial plots. Those at eye level are the most costly, while those at the very bottom or very top of the tier are less expensive. The crypts themselves are most often constructed of concrete, faced with a veneer of granite or marble to lend dignity.

Finally, if neither burial nor aboveground entombment satisfy, there is a space-age potential for the disposal of one's remains. In 1997 a company in Houston, Texas, began offering the ultimate "blastoff" experience. At a current cost of $5,300, a "symbolic portion" of one's cremated remains will be placed into a lipstick-size "flight capsule" and rocketed into Earth orbit. Upon reentering the atmosphere, the flight capsule "harmlessly vaporizes, blazing like a shooting star in final tribute."

The Houston company also advertises flights of one's remains to the moon for lunar orbit and into deep space for an infinite journey. Each of these services is priced at $12,500. They include an invitation to the launch event for family members and friends, a video of the event, and a memorial to the deceased on the company's Web site. Flights are scheduled at various times throughout the year for those who have dreamed of voyaging into space, if only as vestiges of their former selves.

6

Final Resting Places:
Carved in Stone

The ancient Britons are said to have dragged heavy boulders to place atop burial sites as a means of weighing down the ghost of the deceased. They and other early peoples also made it a practice to pile heaps of stones over a grave to keep animal and human predators away.

Whatever the origin of the stone grave marker, it would in time became a memorial and also a means of giving information about the deceased. Gravestones also tell us, through their symbols and sayings, a great deal about the attitudes toward death during the period of the person's life.

Visiting an old New England graveyard of the 1600s and 1700s, one is struck over and over again by the recurring symbols of death carved on the stones. Probably the most common among them is a human skull flanked by a pair of wings. The winged skull expresses two ideas in one: The earthly body is to become a skeleton, but the soul is to fly heavenward on powerful wings.

Here sleeps in peace

HERE LYES Ŷ BODY OF
SARAH STONE
WIFE TO SAMUEL
STONE AGED 63
YEARS DIED OCTOBER
26 1700

Memory
ILLIAM F

Scythes, crossbones, an hourglass showing time running out are other images of death in early America. The graves of children and young people, whose deaths were so common in those days, had their own special symbols—a lamb or a lily to denote purity or a broken column signifying a life cut off before it had achieved full growth.

Other gravestone carvings might display a butterfly, the sign of resurrection; a shell foretelling a pilgrimage; a willow tree as the image of grief; a wreath for mourning; an angel as the guide to heaven; and cherubs of many kinds, often with wings.

In the garden cemeteries of the 1800s, death markers and monuments tend to celebrate the noble traits of those who rest beneath them. Greek columns bespeak the dignity of the deceased. The laurel designates fame. The palm and the sword imply victory, the lamp knowledge, wheat fruitfulness, and the crown promises the reward of heaven. Along with carvings of the Bible and various renditions of the cross, all of the foregoing symbols may still be found in Christian cemeteries. In Jewish cemeteries, the six-pointed Star of David is the most prominent religious symbol.

In Judaism the practice of erecting a burial marker goes all the way back to the Old Testament. In the Book of Genesis it is written that "Jacob set a pillar on her [Rachel's] grave." Although it was not obligatory among Jews to do so, the custom of placing a carved tombstone on a burial site became increasingly common from the sixteenth century A.D. on. The Jewish gravestone may include both the English and Hebrew names of the deceased, as well as dates of birth and death, and as on most grave markers an epitaph, or memorial inscription. Pictorial symbols, in addition to a Star of David, may include a seven-branch menorah, the candelabrum that represents the seven days of the week that make up the creation in the Old Testament.

It is a Jewish tradition for those who visit a grave site to place a small stone atop the burial marker, as a sign of their regard and remembrance.

Other popular Jewish gravestone symbols are a lamp with a flame, signifying the act of commemoration of the deceased; a pair of stone tablets recalling the Ten Commandments; and the Scroll of the Pentateuch, the first five books of the Old Testament.

Jewish custom calls for a ceremony attending the first viewing of the newly erected tombstone within one year of the person's death. Family and friends return to the cemetery for the unveiling, at which time a cloth covering is removed from the stone and special prayers are said.

Among Muslims who adhere to a strict interpretation of Islamic law, grave sites are kept simple, with a mound of earth and a modest headstone allowing for little in the way of carvings. There are, however, many instances of elaborate mausoleums in the Muslim world, an outstanding example of which is the Taj Mahal at Agra, in northern India. This magnificent domed white-marble tomb, flanked by slender prayer towers known as minarets, stands in a garden of reflecting pools and is decorated with carvings from the Koran, the holy book of Islam.

In other places of the Islamic world, such as Iraq, Iran, and Afghanistan, entire cities have sprung up around tomb monuments of highly revered religious persons. At the same time,

Built by 20,000 workers between 1630 and 1650, the Taj Mahal is one of the most beautiful and costly tombs in the world

A modern cemetery, its grave markers arranged with the impersonality of paving stones, in the interest of efficiency and lower maintenance costs.

ordinary Muslim cemeteries have, in some cases, become home to the living. One example is to be found in Cairo, Egypt, where the poor have made themselves family shelters among the grave markers of the dead.

Today, in the newest memorial parks and the aboveground mausoleums, one searches in vain for the carvings of local folk artists or for the more ambitious efforts of mortuary art sculptors. Most new cemeteries limit or ban standing markers, permitting only a flat stone or bronze plaque to be placed on the grave site. Similarly, the facades of aboveground crypts offer room for little more than the names and dates of the deceased, robbing them of any extended form of religious, cultural, or individual expression.

Afterwords

Roaming through the cemeteries of an earlier day, one is struck by the touching and the troubling, the whimsical and the humorous epitaphs of both the little known and the famous. Some of these tombstones inscriptions were self written. Probably best known among them is that of Benjamin Franklin, who said: "In this world, nothing is certain but death and taxes."

A number of years before his death, Franklin penned his epitaph for the amusement of friends. After he died, it was inscribed on a tablet placed near his actual gravestone—which bore only his name and that of his wife—in Philadelphia's Christ Church Burial Ground.

THE BODY OF
B. FRANKLIN, PRINTER,
LIKE THE COVER OF AN OLD BOOK,
ITS CONTENTS TORN OUT,
AND STRIPT OF ITS LETTERING & GILDING,
LIES HERE, FOOD FOR WORMS.

But the Work shall not be lost,
For it will, as he believ'd,
appear once more
In a new and more elegant Edition
Corrected and improved
By the Author.

Poets have often written their own epitaphs. John Gay, author of the English satire on London life, *The Beggar's Opera*, who died in 1732, composed the following lines for his tomb in Westminster Abbey:

Life is a jest; and all things show it,
I thought so once; but now I know it.

And the American poet Robert Frost, who died in 1963, expressed a bitterness in his epitaph that surprised many of the readers of his popular and well-loved work. We learn from Frost's epitaph how troubled he was by the twists of fate that took from him three of his children, while still in their infancy or youth, as well as his wife, leaving him a widower for the last twenty-five years of his life.

On Frost's death, his gravestone in the cemetery of the First Congregational Church in Bennington, Vermont, was inscribed with the single line:

I had a lover's quarrel with the world.

Other New England gravestones seem to have taken an astonishingly lighthearted view of death in marriage. An inscription in a churchyard in Burlington, Vermont, its author unknown, reads:

She lived with her husband fifty years,
And died in the confident hope
of a better life.

And another, in Burlington, Massachusetts, states:

Sacred to the memory of Anthony Drake,
Who died for peace and quietness sake;
His wife was constantly scoldin' and scoffin'
So he sought for repose in a twelve dollar coffin.

Lastly, among those disillusioned with marriage, there is the "Tired Woman's Epitaph," also of unknown authorship, which tells the passerby in no uncertain terms:

Don't mourn for me now,
Don't mourn for me never;
I'm going to do nothing
For ever and ever.

Accidental deaths, too, are treated with remarkable wit. From Kent, England, comes this warning:

Don't attempt to climb a tree,
For that's what caused the death of me.

And in Enosburg, Vermont, we come across this tribute to the unfortunate Anna:

Here lies the body of our Anna
Done to death by a banana.
It wasn't the fruit that laid her low
But the skin of the thing that made her go.

Mike O'Day, whose old tombstone carving indicates that he died in a much earlier time, might well have been one of the automobile drivers of today, for it reads:

HERE LIES THE BODY OF MIKE O'DAY
WHO DIED MAINTAINING HIS RIGHT OF WAY.
HIS RIGHT WAS CLEAR, HIS WILL WAS STRONG,
BUT HE'S JUST AS DEAD AS IF HE'D BEEN WRONG.

Nor can we forget the epitaphs of the gunslingers of the Old West, as represented by the following from a grave in the town of Tombstone, Arizona:

HERE LIES LESTER MOORE
FOUR SLUGS FROM A FORTY-FOUR
NO LES, NO MORE.

Finally, for sheer silliness, here is this one from Skaneateles, New York:

UNDERNEATH THIS PILE OF STONES
LIES ALL THAT'S LEFT OF SALLY JONES.
HER NAME WAS BRIGGS, IT WAS NOT JONES,
BUT JONES WAS USED TO RHYME WITH STONES.

Humorous inscriptions on tombstones and witty remarks, even in the face of death, are a tribute to the human capacity to adapt to the inevitable.

Benjamin Franklin wasn't the only one to wink at death. All sorts of people have come up with choice words on the subject. Some were deathbed quips, while others were fanciful suggestions for tombstone inscriptions that were never actually carved in stone.

When George Bernard Shaw, the Irish-born playwright, lay dying in 1950 at the advanced age of ninety-four he took a remarkably philosophical point of view. "I knew," he remarked matter-of-factly, "that if I stayed around long enough something like this would happen."

Oscar Wilde was yet another Irish-born wit and playwright. But unlike his countryman Shaw, Wilde lived a short and chaotic life. When he died in Paris at the age of forty-six, he was down on his luck, in debt to his friends, and suffering from a fatal ear infection. He was also very dissatisfied with the hideously furnished rented rooms in which he was living. Glancing around at the wallpaper in the chamber where he was confined to bed, Wilde was heard to murmur: "This wallpaper is killing me. One of us has got to go!"

Ideas for imaginary tombstone inscriptions have sprung to the minds of many who found enjoyment in exercising their wit when it came to the prospect of death.

Robert Benchley, the American humorist, who died in 1945, suggested that his grave marker read: "This is all over my head." And the famed novelist and short-story writer, Ernest Hemingway, voted for: "Pardon me for not getting up."

Probably one of the shortest of all memorials that were never carved in stone was American writer Dorothy Parker's offering: "Excuse my dust." The witty Miss Parker, who died in 1967, also penned a verse about suicide that went as follows:

"GUNS AREN'T LAWFUL;
NOOSES GIVE;
GAS SMELLS AWFUL;
YOU MIGHT AS WELL LIVE."

*H*umorous last words, somber deathbed requests, weary or lighthearted remarks intended for one's tombstone—all of these represent responses to the inevitable fact of life—death.

It took Phineas T. Barnum, the greatest circus showman of his day, to insist on looking beyond the grave. He wanted to know what the world was going to say about him after he died.

Barnum, who was born in Bethel, Connecticut, in 1810, started out by exhibiting all sorts of oddities to the public, ranging from a midget called General Tom Thumb to an enormous elephant named Jumbo. Later he organized his circus, which he grandly described as "The Greatest Show on Earth" and began touring it in his own chain of railroad cars. Wealth and fame were his, as he boldly promoted his attractions by means of a kind of advertising that he unashamedly called ballyhoo.

Barnum was immensely proud of his achievements and when, in 1891, he sensed that his final days were approaching, he made an unusual request. He wanted to see his newspaper obituary before he died.

To Barnum's delight, the *New York Sun* complied and on March 24, 1891, it printed the entire four columns that it had held in readiness in anticipation of his demise. The *Sun* even ran a headline calling attention to Barnum's request: "Great and only Barnum. He wanted to read his obituary. Here it is."

With deep satisfaction, the ailing Barnum read the very words that would remain with the rest of the world once he was no more. Two weeks later, on April 7, 1891, he died at his home in Bridgeport, Connecticut, content in the knowledge that his genius for show business had been preserved for posterity.

Barnum's desire to read his own obituary may also be seen as an attempt to cheat death. Even the fourteen days that he lived beyond the public review of his life and his accomplish-ments gave him the illusion that he had somehow extended his span on earth, or even returned from the grave.

Perhaps this is the illusion that we all seek, for life is such a vital force that it hardly seems unreasonable, the closer we come to it, to push away the concept of death.

Source Notes

Gathering material for a book on such a universal subject as death requires reaching into the broadest possible range of sources. In addition to the titles listed in the bibliography, I have gleaned material from collections of folklore, poetry, quotations, and signs and symbols; from general encyclopedias and from mythological, biblical, religious, historical, and biographical reference works.

I have built a file of relevant matter from newspapers, periodicals, and television. Information of the moment on cryogenics, the space-launching of cremated remains, and on the newest developments in cemetery design and mausoleum architecture has been obtained from the Internet.

I have also derived material for *Dying to Know* from research done on my previously published books, particularly *Slumps, Grunts, and Snickerdoodles: What Colonial America Ate and Why*; *Piñatas and Paper Flowers: Holidays of the Americas in English and Spanish*; and *Mummies, Tombs, and Treasure: Secrets of Ancient Egypt* (all Clarion Books).

Lila Perl

Bibliography

Arbeiter, Jean and Linda D. Cirino. *Permanent Addresses: A Guide to the Resting Places of Famous Americans.* New York: M. Evans & Co., 1983.

Ariès, Philippe. *The Hour of Our Death.* New York: Knopf, 1981.

Dempsey, David. *The Way We Die: An Investigation of Death and Dying in America Today.* New York: Macmillan, 1975.

Donaldson, Norman and Betty Donaldson. *How Did They Die?* New York: Greenwich House/Crown, 1980.

Eills, Nancy and Parker Hayden. *Here Lies America: A Collection of Notable Graves.* New York: Hawthorn Books, 1978.

Garrison, Webb. *Strange Facts About Death.* Nashville, TN: Abingdon, 1978.

Jones, Constance. *R.I.P.: The Complete Book of Death and Dying*. New York: HarperCollins, 1997.

Lynch, Thomas. *The Undertaking: Life Studies from the Dismal Trade*. New York: W. W. Norton, 1997.

McDowell, Peggy and Richard E. Meyer. *The Revival Styles in American Memorial Art*. Bowling Green, OH: Bowling Green State University Popular Press, 1994.

Mitford, Jessica. *The American Way of Death*. New York: Simon & Schuster, 1963.

————. *The American Way of Death Revisited*. New York: Alfred A. Knopf, 1998.

Panati, Charles. *Panati's Extraordinary Endings of Practically Everything and Everybody*. New York: Harper & Row, 1989.

Prochnik, Leon. *Endings: Death, Glorious and Otherwise, As Faced by Ten Outstanding Figures of Our Time*. New York: Crown, 1980.

Turner, Ann Warren. *Houses for the Dead: Burial Customs Through the Ages*. New York: David McKay, 1976.

Wallechinsky, David, Irving Wallace, and Amy Wallace. *The Book of Lists*. New York: Morrow, 1977.

Wallechinsky, David and Amy Wallace. *The Book of Lists: The '90's Edition*. Boston: Little Brown, 1993.

Index

About the Author

Lila Perl has written more than fifty books for young people and adults, both fiction and nonfiction. Her nonfiction titles have dealt mainly with social history, family memoir, biography, and cultural and background studies of African nations, China, and Latin America. She has written on subjects as diverse as foods and food customs, genealogy, Egyptian mummies, and the Holocaust.

Two of her books have been honored with ALA Notable Awards, and she has received a Boston Globe-Horn Book Award. In addition to its 1997 ALA Notable and YALSA/ALA citations, *Four Perfect Pebbles* was named a "Best of the Bunch" selection by the Sydney Taylor Awards Committee.

Nine of Lila Perl's nonfiction titles have been cited NCSS-CBC Notable Children's Trade Books in the Field of Social Studies. They include *Mummies, Tombs, and Treasure*; *The Great Ancestor Hunt*; and *It Happened in America: True Stories from the Fifty States*.

Lila Perl lives in Beechhurst, New York.